Stained Glass

Music for the Eye

Robert and Jill Hill
Hans Halberstadt

The Scrimshaw Press
1976

© copyright 1976 by The Scrimshaw Press

Library of Congress Cataloging in Publication Data

Hill, Robert, 1939–
   Stained glass: music for the eye.

   1. Glass painting and staining—History.   2. Glass
painting and staining—Technique.   I. Hill, Jill, 1944–
II. Halberstadt, Hans.   III. Title.
NK5306.H55   748.5   76–27286
ISBN 0–912020–55–5
ISBN 0–912020–45–8 pbk.

All photographs, except as noted,
    are by Hans Halberstadt.

The Scrimshaw Press
6040 Claremont Avenue
Oakland, California 94618

INTRODUCTION

WHILE THE ENERGY of light seems to penetrate to the very nature of matter, giving to all things seen their visual cadences and harmonies, the *substance* of light is elusive . . . forever moving with the sun and shadows, as if it lived and breathed without time or space.

But it is in man's nature to want to capture and hold beauty. By adorning ourselves with precious stones, placing them in ornate settings, or arranging them in harmonious patterns, we give light something to play upon, and create for our eyes the pleasure that music gives the ear. The stained glass artist is composer-conductor of a visual symphony; light and color are his instruments. Some

colors dominate, while others appear to be listening, quietly waiting for a change in light or a movement in the trees behind the window, waiting for their turn to add fullness to the composition with their own particular tone or pitch.

There is nothing quite like marveling at a series of stained glass windows in a darkened space, immersing oneself in the qualities of design and painted detail, and then suddenly being enveloped in an overwhelming burst of color as the sun moves from behind a cloud. The experience provides the viewer an excitement for which there are no words. If our book can convey even a portion of this excitement, we will be satisfied.

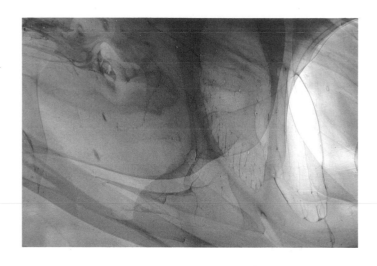

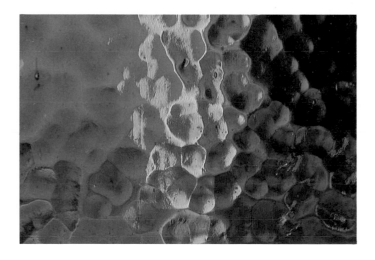

Varieties of visual experience—some of the choices available to contemporary glass artists : upper left, mouth-blown streaked glass ; lower left, machine-made hammered glass ; above, seedy-clear antique glass.

ORIGINS

"Light is the most noble of natural phenomena, the least material, the closest approximation to pure form."

—Otto Von Simson
The Gothic Cathedral

THE ATTRACTION TO the control of light and color is not new, although we keep finding new ways to express it. In ancient temples of the Far East, early forms of colored glass were used as jewellike highlights, set in screens of alabaster. The walls of the Hagia Sophia, the great temple built in Constantinople in the sixth century, were pierced with a closely-spaced ring of grilled windows that glowed with nuggets of glass set in the transparent lace network.

One of the oldest surviving leaded windows, dating from the ninth century, was found buried in a cemetery at Séry-les-Mézières in northern France. In ochre and olive green glass painted with black pigment, it depicted a Greek cross, with the letters alpha and omega in the lower corners. (It was destroyed in 1918.) Excavations at Lorsch and Magdeburg, in Germany, have unearthed remains of early pictorial windows that date from the ninth and tenth centuries.

Most historians agree, however, that the oldest complete examples of what we now know as stained glass are the windows in the clerestory of Augsburg Cathedral, completed in the early twelfth century. The monks of Tengersee who created these windows used ideas and techniques that were already highly developed. The figures depicted are stylized, almost modern-looking. The eyebrows, nose, and mouth, for example, are connected in a nearly continuous line, reminiscent of oriental Sumi painting. The elliptically-shaped eyes appear to stare at a space in the center of the forehead. The style is Byzantine, of the Hellenic tradition and, unlike most of the later Gothic stained glass, these windows have a dominant green hue that gives them a rich, luminescent quality against the sky.

Perhaps the greatest charm of the windows is their age. The pitting of the glass, the tiny depressions on the surface, filled with hundreds of

Birth of a medium—a window from Augsburg Cathedral, dating from about 1135 A.D. (Photo from Deutsche Kunstverlag, Munich.)

8

years of dust, gives a shading effect; and the accumulation of dust around the edges of each glass piece makes their centers glow with greater intensity. (This natural corrosion is a feature some modern glass painters try painstakingly to reproduce with iron oxide mattes.) The years have also brought an accumulation of lead reinforcement for cracked pieces, and time has added immeasurably to the character of the windows, enhancing their mosaic quality, making them truly "windows of miraculous light."

Where did it come from, the crafting of these marvelous glass mosaics? The history of their creation is indefinite in origin, arising out of the intellectual climate and growing religious fervor of the years before the eleventh century, and appearing simultaneously in several European countries. With the spread of Christianity, churches became centers of learning. Filled with mosaics, sculptures, and frescoes, these churches were classrooms as well as visual feasts for the education of the townspeople in biblical matters.

Each artistic activity was so closely related to and influenced by the others that it is difficult to determine in what form new ideas first appeared. Pre-Gothic manuscript illuminations, with figures depicted in overlapping flat planes of firmly drawn contours, were filled in with bright colors —a form of illustration highly adaptable to glass. The craft of making stained glass windows was probably also influenced by the stonemason and goldsmith trades and by the art of Venetian enameling, which was introduced in France in the tenth century.

With the beginnings of Gothic architecture in France, glass techniques developed rapidly. Religious structures were becoming more skeletal, and clerestory windows grew to vast size, demanding to be filled with light and color. To complete these gigantic undertakings, craftsmen erected tent-workshops in the shadows of church walls. The windows were made on these building sites, with the glass workers often locating their furnaces on the forest's edge. When a task was completed, the tent-workshops were packed up and moved to other towns.

Skilled glass craftsmen later branched off to wander throughout Europe, stopping when and where work was plentiful. Not until the fourteenth century do we find, as part of the general artistic vigor of the Renaissance, the establishment of glass studios in fixed locations.

EARLY TECHNIQUES

EARLY IN THE TWELFTH century, the monk Theophilus recorded the ancient glass-making formula: two parts beech and bracken ash (yielding potash, an alkaline base) and one part river sand, washed free of earthly particles. He explained that this mixture, when heated, first assumed a pale green color; as heating was prolonged, it acquired a warm purplish cast which Theophilus described as "flesh-color" (probably due to the presence of manganese in the ash).

Further colors were once thought to have been obtained by grinding up shards of glass from antique mosaics, but the source of supply must have been quickly exhausted. Suger, Abbot of Saint-Denis, is said to have boasted of grinding up sapphires in order to obtain the blue coloring of his glass, a wonderfully unlikely story. Glass was usually colored by the addition of various metallic oxides and salts to the molten ash-and-sand mixture during the process of fusion. The colors obtained depended on the type of metal used and the temperature to which it was taken. In the beginning, the colors were limited to blue, red, purple, green, and yellow.

A beautiful azure blue, very pure, of high intensity, and most plentiful during the twelfth century, was developed through the use of cobalt oxides coming from the mineral ores of Saxony and Bohemia.

Red, the most difficult color to handle during the process of fusion, was derived by throwing copper filings into the basic glass mixture along with flakes of iron that acted as a reducing agent. These reds were sometimes so richly intense that light could not penetrate the entire thickness of the glass, and often the color was limited to a thin red layer "flashed" onto one surface of clear glass. This flashing or plating process was later extended to other colors and eventually used to advantage by nineteenth century craftsmen, who etched away areas of the flashed color with hydrofluoric acid.

The natural mineral ores of France provided most of the oxides needed for coloring. Copper dioxide was used to obtain greens, with some cobalt often added to give the green a bluish tint. Purple was produced by mixing manganese oxide with small amounts of iron oxide and copper shavings. Yellow was created from sesquioxide of iron or dioxide of manganese.

Large fireproof clay pots were used to fuse the metallic oxides with clear glass at red-hot temperatures, and then the glassblower set to work. Gathering the molten glass on the end of his blowing-tube, he blew the liquid into a rough sphere, and, by swinging and twisting, obtained a cylindrical shape. This was cut at both ends, opened along its axis, and allowed to cool. It was then placed in an annealing oven and reheated, causing the glass to flatten out on a stone, forming a small sheet of uneven thickness. In the case of red flashed glass, the blower dipped his pipe into the molten color, and blew a bubble which he then dipped into molten white glass. It was worked as before, but the resulting glass had a thin layer of color on one surface only, allowing the rich translucence of the red.

Made in this way, medieval glass—like today's "antique glass"—had considerable variations of thickness, causing greater and lesser intensities of color within each sheet. A harmonious union of flaws and irregularities, reams and air bubbles, the glass refracted the sun's rays, making the now-colored light dance and sparkle.

Having been allowed to cool, the colored glass sheets were placed on a large wooden table coated with whitewash. Since the medieval artists hadn't the benefit of large sheets of paper, this table probably served as the location not only of guidelines for glass cutting, but also of cartoon lines for glass painting. (The term "cartoon" denotes a full-size black and white drawing taken from a small-scale drawing.) For cutting, a thin line of sheep or cow urine was applied to the glass, and a red-hot dividing iron was placed along the line, causing the glass to crack. Any rough edges were then chewed or smoothed away with grozing irons that resemble today's pliers. Such primitive cutting methods severely limited the maximum size of the glass pieces, and often as many as four hundred pieces were required to the square yard.

The cut pieces were then arranged on the table and glass painters, using as paint a mixture of iron or copper oxides and pulverized glass mixed with urine or wine, traced the details of facial features, drapery folds, and ornamentation onto the glass, following the cartoon lines. The paint mixture, a dark grayish brown in hue, was used to outline and emphasize portions of the images, with compensations for the distance from which they would be seen. Colored paint was not added to colored glass; rather, light was blocked out by negative areas, thereby leaving colored shapes.

The glass was then fired in a furnace to fuse glass and paint. After cooling, the glass was usually painted again—this time with a thinner layer of the same paint mixture—and smoothed while wet with wide badger-hair brushes until each piece was covered with a thin layer of paint (called a matte). This thin pigment was allowed to dry and was then carefully scraped away from specific areas where more light was needed to penetrate and reveal pure or subdued colors. Us-ing this technique, the artists obtained modeling and shading effects where depth was required. Color could be made to appear more intense by a darkening of the surrounding areas; excessively brilliant colors could be subdued by stippling the paint. This second painting process was again fired, and the numerous pieces were placed once more on the cartoon, to be joined with lead strips.

Prior to the thirteenth century, pure molten lead for joining the glass pieces was cast in hollow reeds or poured into grooves in long, thin boxes. From the thirteenth century until fairly recently, lead was cast into metal molds in a solid form, and grooved by a wheel to obtain the necessary channels, or was extruded by a hand-cranked machine. Teeth marks are evident on both sides of the core in the latter case, where the gears seized the lead to pull it through the extruder.

Each glass piece, placed in its appropriate position, was inserted into its lead channel and soldered at the joints until a panel of predetermined size could be lifted in one piece. A putty-like compound was then hand-rubbed into the areas between the lead flanges and the surface of the glass, making it weatherproof and providing additional strength as well.

The completed windows were made up of a number of panels set between iron crossbars, additionally supported with tied and soldered small square rods fashioned by the resident blacksmiths. Larger windows of the late thirteenth and the fourteenth centuries, too broad to allow the glass sufficient support, were divided by stone or wooden lancets and tracery patterns.

The manufacture of glass today provides a broader color range than the medieval artists were able to obtain. But to this day, the character and technique of the stained glass craft have remained fundamentally unchanged, giving today's viewer an immediate link with the past. The contemporary glass artist utilizes centuries-old methods and principles, insisting, as did the medieval artist, on light as the first consideration.

BY THE TWELFTH CENTURY stained glass had emerged as an integral part of Gothic architecture, and the twelfth and thirteenth centuries, known as the golden age of stained glass, yielded what are generally assumed to be the finest windows ever produced. The techniques of the craft were by this time far advanced, and craftsmen had developed the ability to solve and compensate for problems of scale. Windows were designed and made for a particular location, with an eye toward the quantity and quality of light they would receive. Each small feature, particularly in the figures, was made for the angle and distance from which it would be seen, giving the forms an abstract character all their own. (The details are well worth seeing if you ever are afforded the opportunity to climb up for a closer view.)

One of the rose windows of Chartres Cathedral. Medieval artists were severely limited in their color range but limitless in their imagination.

In the early Gothic churches, the windows were luminous colored walls filling the spaces between the piers, where once there had been walls of murals and mosaics. The result was an atmosphere of quiet meditation, with the glass becoming a vehicle for transforming the interior space into glowing imagery . . . a visual, almost mystical experience for the beholder.

The work of this period may well be described as symbolic abstraction—subject matter easily understood by the illiterate. It became more than mere naturalism and decoration, however, for the artist was devoted to the nature of the materials he used, integrating his forms with them. A conceptual expression of love that was felt rather than pictured, the stained glass windows became "true" in their expression and were a reflection of their creators.

The pioneer of the Gothic movement, Suger, Abbot of Saint-Denis, was instrumental in commissioning and supervising the work on many of the early windows. In his *Livre sur son administration* he states that his purpose was "to direct thought by material means toward that which is immaterial." So great was his enthusiasm that he had his portrait done as a small figure lying prostrate at the feet of the Virgin in one of the windows of the North Chapel at Saint-Denis. And after the installation of his "windows of miraculous light," he went so far as to hire a master craftsman to see to their maintenance and preservation.

Chartres : panels below the rose window on page 14. The intense blues and reds, juxtaposed, seem to advance and recede through a third dimension.

16

Thirteenth-century Western Europe saw the building of magnificent cathedrals, with windows that spanned increasingly large openings. The reconstruction of Chartres Cathedral (after the fire of 1194) particularly reflected the climate of "cathedral glory." Artists and clergy spent thirty years designing and constructing Chartres's one hundred seventy-three windows. The result is a breathtaking monument of stone and light. No other cathedral possesses such a wealth of stained glass, and Chartres appears to be alive with ever-changing color: reds and oranges during the morning hours, and more of the darker hues in the slanting rays of the setting sun. The celestial blues give the illusion of non-substance, while the deep, intense reds appear to be closer to us, considerably forward of the strong blues, giving the windows a shimmering, ethereal quality, as if matter had been transformed. Negative space, in the form of paint and lead, was used wisely and generously; this allows some colors to merge harmoniously with one another while others seem to dance and vibrate with the movement of the sun. As evening approaches, the irridescent jewels of color begin to dull, receding into an atmosphere of peace and tranquillity.

[Continued on page 21]

*Canterbury Cathedral, England, circa 1200. Stained glass
windows improve with age. Centuries of wind and weather pit
the glass, and a gradual accumulation of dirt creates a
natural patina.*

Detail of a window in Cologne Cathedral circa 1250. Glass artists of this period began to make larger windows and use lighter colors than their predecessors.

19

A window in Cologne Cathedral . . .

20

The influence of the Chartres windows spread throughout Europe, with some of the same decorative backgrounds and color concepts persisting in other great cathedrals: Bourges (1235), Le Mans (1254), Tours (1255), and Sainte-Chapelle in Paris (1243). For two more centuries, stained glass craftsmen refined technical processes and developed new directions in style. While these were years of exceptional merit, architectural activity began to decline, and with it the demand for stained glass. Windows still exemplified the expressive energy of the golden age, but the geometric framework of earlier designs no longer dominated the compositions. Figures became larger in proportion to the whole, and relief-like in their painted shading, giving them a "colored" perspective.

In architecture, there was an increasing demand for more interior light. Windows became higher and wider, with thinner and more intricate traceries. Glass craftsmen, now working with lighter colors, gave greater attention to painted detail. In the absence of strong color, negative space became more important visually. The emphasis was shifting away from the glass craftsman and toward the hand facility of the glass *painter*. In England particularly, the lack of strong sunlight dictated a choice of colors away from the strong blues and reds toward yellows and neutral tones. The discovery of a rich golden-yellow stain accentuated this change, and the artist, for the first time, could obtain two colors on the same piece of glass without the necessity of a dividing lead strip. (The stain, produced by using silver nitrate, is a salt incompatible with the iron oxides in glass paint and is applied to the reverse side of the glass and fired at a fairly low temperature.) This discovery caused a small revolution in the craft and heavily influenced glass painting developments.

The fifteenth century found the skilled glass painters in a dominant position, elevated to a level far above that of the glass craftsmen. The painted image on glass, in an age of realism and

[Continued on page 33]

Above, a detail of a nineteenth-century French window : enamel on clear glass (James Wagner collection). Right, an early twentieth-century American window : rondels with lead overlay. (Perry Studio collection.)

22

Early twentieth-century American free-hanging panel: sheet lead cut-out overlaid on glass in an attempt to avoid the use of glass paint. (Brusey Studio collection.)

Above, a detail of the window opposite : a nineteenth-century
English window that temporarily immortalized its subject.
With every new election, a new portrait was quickly painted
on a piece of clear glass and the portrait of the predecessor
was removed from view.
Left, a detail of a nineteenth-century English window,
showing prolific use of yellow stain. (James Wagner collection.)

These silk-screened hanging medallions of the early twentieth century were made in Seattle from glass pieces produced by assembly line in England. (Perry Studio collection.) Opposite, a new use of the old medallion idea.

26

Above, an eighteenth-century English piece salvaged from a damaged window shows an extensive use of yellow stain. (Perry Studio collection.) Right, a nineteenth-century English window. (Brusey Studio collection.)

An early twentieth-century American window, painted with brown oxide paint. (Perry Studio collection.)

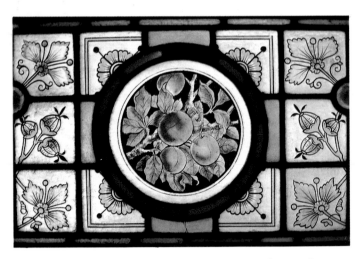

Two eighteenth-century English windows, done with enamels, stains, and oxides. (James Wagner collection.)

An English window from the nineteenth century. It was common for donors of windows to have their portraits included in the windows they sponsored. (Perry Studio collection.)

A nineteenth-century English window, one of our favorites. (Perry Studio collection.)

31

Cooper House, Santa Cruz, California. This open-air skylight, made from opalescent glass, spans a gap between two buildings. Opalescent skylights were produced by the hundreds in America in the early twentieth century.

over-refinement, took precedence over the natural raw beauty of color. The designer turned to the beauty of nature, and his window borders flowed with painted foliage. The artist painted figures to emphasize individual personality, with donors themselves often depicted striving toward the divine. Artists signed their windows for the first time. The older styles of painting on colored glass were declining in favor of the use of nearly colorless glass windows to show off the artist's talent as a *painter*. Lead lines were treated as an evil necessity.

The old techniques were all but obliterated during the seventeenth and eighteenth centuries, and they came to be considered a lost art. Stained glass had become an independent art form; windows were completely pictorial, and the essential tics with architecture were forgotten. The deterioration of the craft was largely a product of what English critic Sir Herbert Read called the "false aesthetics of glass painting." This attempt by the glass painter to think in terms of canvas painting techniques rather than the transformation of light was furthered by the introduction of a Swiss-developed colored enamel paint for glass. (It is likely that the term "stained glass," actually a misnomer, was adopted at the time of this new development.) The new paint found its most enthusiastic support in France, where recognized canvas painters were commissioned to adapt their talents to glass, often with implausible results. The merits of this trend, carried through to the present day, are the subject of furious debate among contemporary glass artists.

The stained glass of this period represented the spirit of the era and should be appreciated from that standpoint. While the windows produced can hardly be described with excitement, they are beautiful in their way. The English designer, John Piper, terms them "interesting manifestations of their own age," meeting the client's and architect's expectation of well-made products of the establishment. But a revival, fortunately, was in the making. *[Continued on page 45]*

Winchester House, San Jose, California, artist unknown.
The center of each flower is slag glass (chunks knocked out of
the glassmaker's barrels at the end of each working day).
Note the subtle gradations of yellow stain in the background.

34

In Golden Gate Villa, Santa Cruz, California, an early twentieth-century American Art Nouveau window using opalescent glass.

This turn-of-the-century window, removed from a residence in San Jose, is typical of the opalescent glass windows of the period.

In another Golden Gate Villa room, an early twentieth-century American window in the Victorian style. The entire center of the window is painted with enamels.

Morrow's Nut House, Santa Cruz. A contemporary use of an
early twentieth-century design style, with an extensive
use of opalescent glass to accommodate artificial lighting.
(Artist: John Forbes.)

A nineteenth-century American window—acid etching on red-flashed-on-white glass. The difficult dark-to-light values required several acid baths before the proper shading was obtained. (Perry Studio collection.)

*A nineteenth-century American window, with
a design taken from an ancient Chinese print,
using the acid-etching technique. The detail
on the right was shot into direct sunlight,
using a filter. (Brusey Studio collection.)*

40

Bevelled glass is soft crystal glass, hand-ground on a flat wheel so that it refracts light, creating colored prisms. The process of bevelling is slow, painstaking, and exacting, and every craftsman who produces bevelled glass has his own preferred degree of angle.

In the early twentieth century, a bevelling machine was invented, and the glass began to be used extensively for decoration combined with maximum translucency. Its greatest popularity was in the Pacific Northwest, where lack of constant sunlight is a problem. But the cost of bevelled glass is high, and its use now is limited. This example comes from the Winchester House, San Jose.

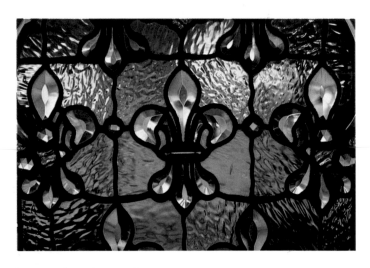

Again, from the Winchester House, San Jose.

A bevelled-glass panel found in a storage shed, date and artist unknown.

*Garden-variety bevelled-glass door panels
from a boarding house in Seattle, Washington.*

44

The nineteenth and early twentieth centuries were times of transition and change. There was a new demand for construction and renovation of Gothic structures. With this new-old activity came a call for pure color in glass, a need recognized and publicized in the late nineteenth century by Viollet-Le-Duc, French Minister of Public Monuments, who studied Gothic architectural style and recorded his findings for use in the restoration of French cathedrals. Viollet's writings included an analysis of stained glass window making and his own color radiation theory. Craftsmen, rediscovering the craft's ancient techniques with an eye toward the unsurpassed beauty of the great medieval windows, returned to the use of pot metal (glass and metallic oxide fused in a melting pot). Formulas were revived and experimentation produced new irridescent glass colors. Slowly the heavy influence of the picture-window with meaningless embellishment gave way to the use of lead for color area separations. The glazier, exemplified by England's William Morris, again became as important as the glass painter, and lead once more became an integral part of window design. The revival was partially underway.

Even so, early attempts to return to the true nature of the medium were hindered by the lack of approval of various academies of the arts and by the commercialism that resulted from the Industrial Revolution. Established nineteenth-century stained glass studios catalogued standardized designs, utilizing production-line techniques to compensate for rising costs. Improvements in the craft came slowly, but are obvious when one looks back to the works of the previous two centuries. The "lost art" legend was beginning to die.

Germany was perhaps the most logical of the European countries to nourish a radical movement in stained glass. Charles Connick toured there in 1936: "Stained glass abounds in Germany. We found examples in nearly every cathedral and church we entered, though we rarely felt that anyone cared very deeply about it. But we did find in many hot and garish windows bits of true blue glass that we labeled twelfth century." By the time of reconstruction at the end of World War II, German architectural thought was in the midst of an extraordinarily broad reform. Walter Gropius and the influential Bauhaus school, opposing the traditional concept of a window as no more than a hole in a wall, regarded the wall it-self as a curtain—a climate barrier able to reflect and transmit light. Made an integral part of this school of thought, stained glass became a basic element in German post-war architecture. Many of the hot and garish windows described by Connick were replaced with almost colorless linear windows. This design style, still the direction of German stained glass today, is a structural, un-emotional discipline with a distinction shown between glass as a pure substance and glass as a treated surface. In the Church of Maria Königin, in Cologne, for example, one entire wall of delicate leaf patterns, done in textured machined and blown glass, varies in tones of grays and tinted whites. For all its massiveness, the window-wall vibrates and shimmers with life, dancing as light filters through the trees outside. Conspicuously absent in its design is any hint of the glass painter's former dominance. (See pp. 54-55.)

[Continued on page 58]

Contemporary designs in old traceries. These, in Cologne Cathedral, use antique glass. Above, a detail; on the facing page, a full window.

St. Ursula's Church, Cologne, Germany.
This page and opposite : two windows in the
same church—both examples of contemporary
German design, one restrained, one exuberant.
(Artist : Wilhelm Büschulte.)

49

August Pieper Haus, Aachen. This design is built upon obvious lead lines and the use of almost colorless glass. The numerous flashed white pieces are used on the theory that the eye should stop at the window rather than travel through it. (Artist: Ludwig Schaffrath.)

50

A church window in Köln-Mengenich, Cologne. On the facing page, a detail. (Artist: Ludwig Schaffrath.)

Köln-Mengenich, Cologne. A detail of a larger window.
Opposite : yet another. (Artist : Schaffrath.)

Church of Maria Königin, Cologne. This window of mechanically textured glass and antique glass is an excellent example of the Bauhaus window-as-wall concept. Above, a detail; on the facing page, a full view. (Artists: Dominikus Böhm and Heinz Bienefeld.)

54

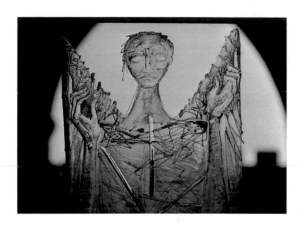

The west wall of Coventry Cathedral in England, done in incised glass by John Hutton. In the background are the ruins of the old cathedral, destroyed by bombing during World War II.

While German glass artists struck out in new directions, in France the craft remained under the influence of the glass painter. Producing prolific amounts of heavily painted windows, the country that was once the leading force in stained glass remained caught in the trap of pictorialism. Even today, with notable exceptions such as the accomplishments of the late Gabriel Loire and the late Max Ingraham, a great majority of French work still shows the predominance of painted glass. In the large view, however, this may provide a necessary balance, a check against overly structured glass design.

Meanwhile, the quality of stained glass in the United States was largely the result of a nostalgia in our newly-affluent American society for the opulence of European windows. Succumbing to the idea of European artistic superiority, the larger churches imported their windows (and often still do), limiting American craftsmen to low-budget creations. Those first efforts represented the fundamental principles of the old craft, and primarily secular buildings used heavily colored small pieces of glass set in geometric patterns, with little use of glass painting, mainly due to the cost involved.

In an attempt to completely eliminate the need for painting on glass to resist the brilliant American sunlight, John La Farge developed what is still known as "opalescent" glass. Fairly opaque, the glass has milky streaks of color fused into it, giving it a cloudy appearance. Although La Farge's intentions were honorable, this glass that reflected light as well as transmitting it had an ultimately gloomy effect. The flat subtle color combinations, when well planned, could be used effectively, but often were (and still are) used with poor taste. Emil Frei, an early proponent of modern glass design, abhorred the use of this glass, declaring: "Its fused surface colors, rarely clear and pure, were dominated by questionable combinations of brown-yellows and nondescript greens that would nauseate an artist's color sense." Opalescent glass, however, was something new, something uniquely American, and its popularity swept the country.

Recognizing the potential of this new glass, Louis C. Tiffany combined it with a patented "favrile" glass, producing unique windows and lampshades of the Art Nouveau style that epitomized the sensuous line. His studio was also credited with the invention and prolific use of copper foil covered with solder as a lead replacement to better handle small pieces of glass and curved surfaces.

In an attempt to entirely eliminate glass painting, the Tiffany Studio craftsmen created subtly-colored scenes with a specialized glass used for drapery and shading. Glass paint was used only to add necessary details to flesh tones and for inscriptions. Tiffany Studio advertising declared: "As all our windows are built in accordance with the mosaic theory, without the intervention of paint, stains, or enamels, they are practically indestructible and will not corrode, peel or fade."

While there was no question as to the quality of workmanship, the stained glass craft was still largely at the mercy of the pseudo-Gothic architectural style, and little could be done for the craft's advancement as a creative expression. The advent of the Great Depression seemed a threat to the very existence of stained glass in the United States. It was, in fact (as was World War II in Germany) an opportunity for change. The sudden economic downswing resulted in a necessary architectural simplicity, and did away with the meaningless, over-zealous decoration that had allowed mediocre glassmen to hide a lack of talent and imagination. The stained glass artist was left face-to-face with his creative ability.

NEW CONCEPTS

THE STAINED GLASS CRAFT still reels from the effect of hundreds of years of the painter's approach, which treated glass as if it were a canvas. But there is a new and growing respect for the original principles of light and color as first considerations. Given this mood, the need for change and expansion is exemplified by those working with contemporary designs while utilizing traditional techniques, treating the glass in an effort to alter and control the action of light.

If we use the space within a circle as an illustration, on one side is the artist who treats the glass surface in literally every way imaginable. On the other side in the circle is the artist who believes in non-interference with light, allowing the glass to "speak for itself." Within this circle, much like the ancient symbol of Yin and Yang, there is a constant transformation of one force into the other—a constant flow of energy back and forth —each school of thought influencing, restraining,

needing the other. Each side is motivated by a light/color concept basic to the qualities of glass. The stained glass movement in the United States contains both schools, and fluctuates between the two.

To gain some idea of contemporary stained glass direction in the United States, we immersed ourselves in a stained glass patent application file. There were a variety of techniques proposed by those hoping either to reduce costs or improve the quality of today's craft. Patented innovations ranged from ways of joining glass to poured plastic compounds. The character of the glass, in most cases, was to be altered by sagging, fusing, turning strips edgewise, faceting, or crushing—treatments all claiming to cause remarkable light refractions. Our interest ended entirely when we came to "Imitation Glass in Concrete," and we left feeling a little foolish, afraid that we might eventually have uncovered a patent for genuine Tiffany-style window screen kits.

Narcissus Quagliata created these windows for a private residence, using neutral tones to set off the richness of the colored antique glass.

We then met with established stained glass artists working by commission. We found many of their efforts hampered by their client's preconceived ideas of what design "should" be. Occasionally requests challenge the artist's creative ability, but more often he is asked to make innumerable compromises with his own convictions by working in all styles. (We still have haunting personal memories of an early compromise. During a design discussion concerning a residential window, our client disappeared into another room and returned with his pet parrot, which was to be realistically portrayed in greens to match the carpet. He also wanted an opalescent pink background to please his grandmother, and a garish orange in the window's border for brightness. Unfortunately the commission was accepted, and we've loathed parrots ever since.) To resolve these conflicts of integrity, an artist in stained glass will usually try to combine the merits of the client's ideas with as much of himself as possible. He is, after all, approached in the first place because, theoretically, he knows his medium better than anyone else. The contemporary artist who achieves personal success by producing consistently safe windows, retreating behind poor copies of design idioms, merely prolongs the agony endured throughout the history of stained glass. Both he and society suffer by accepting work that is less than sincere in its approach.

Since the essential purpose of stained glass is the refraction and transformation of light, it has been traditionally thought of as an architectural element. But many of today's more innovative artists are seriously working in glass for the purpose of exhibition rather than commission, in an effort to maintain integrity and excellence of workmanship. These people regard their work as a creative statement that can stand on its own, and they feel they have the right to acknowledge and treat it as such. The justification for this opinion lies in the very nature of the artist who must express himself through his materials. In this way, the artist not only comes to renewed self-understanding, but is again reminded of the responsibility of combatting dedication to outmoded forms and ideas.

There are lessons to be learned by this trend in the craft, for with it comes the danger of losing sight of the primary relationship of stained glass to its architectural setting. For example, the city of Bellevue, Washington, recently held a design competition for stained glass windows to be placed in a public building. While there was a formidable front-lighting problem, this nation wide competition resulted in more than eighty submitted designs. Of those entered, very few showed any indication of having been conceived in terms of glass. Even fewer considered the problem of visually integrating the windows with the proposed architecture. While this particular situation lacked the necessary collaboration between architect and artist, it still points out the artist's misconception that a structure must somehow serve to set off his own dreams of beauty. The fact is, the artist's creative image *can* stand out independently, just as each instrument in an orchestra plays its particular score, with the architect/composer pulling the various relationships together into a central idea. Today's architects are giving us vital, challenging secular architecture, ideally suited to harmonize with the creative needs of the artist. Stained glass and architecture, evolving from the same basic source, are both acts of creativity, intuition, understanding, and skill. Each results in a constant flow of ideas, based on standards that come from an individual awareness of values and a past that contains the seeds of continuity.

Continuing our search for new concepts, we met with yet another group of artists, who seem to be pushing toward absolute purity in glass.

Holding the premise that various treatments may somehow suppress the glass's vitality, they design within the framework of glass and lead as given limitations, and are obviously affected by the current German design direction. But herein lies an interesting paradox. Rather than working the glass into a given design, these American artists give the *glass* first consideration and let *it* decide the direction of their composition. The selection of glass for these artists, therefore, becomes a process almost sacramental in nature. In practical necessity, though, the design of a project and its execution are of equal importance. The resulting blend of artist/craftsman may very well indicate a resurgence in the very nature of the craft such as that found during the Gothic revival of the late eighteenth century.

Perhaps a natural extension of the medium within this climate of thought is found in the relatively recent use of inch-thick *dalle-de-verre*, or dalle glass, cast in a concrete or epoxy matrix. In appearance, dalle glass has a basic, organic nature, and glass paint is seldom used to alter its surface. The matrix areas become negative space, blocking the transmission of light, thereby allowing the artist greater opportunity to control the balance of light. While dalle glass can be somewhat limiting in terms of spontaneity, it is well suited to contemporary architecture's natural lighting problems and requirements.

Many artists feel a need to create spontaneously during a work's actual execution. Traditionally, spontaneity in a stained glass window was limited to the design process; the materials used in execution added to or supported the fixed design. We find now that at times the design is more a conceptual idea than a rigid blueprint—an approach that gives the artist greater flexibility. To find anything approaching a unified movement in this direction, we began looking at the seriously aspiring artists still in the early stages of learning the craft. As yet unencumbered by society's idea of what stained glass "ought" to be, undaunted by the craft's portentously rich historical tradition, these newcomers reflect a freshness and an excited, almost blind, enthusiasm. They choose not to hide behind the medium's limitations; instead, they seem consistently to squeeze out those bursts of creativity so necessary to maintaining a spontaneous style. And they carry this trend to its fullest extent, experimenting with stains, acids, pure color, paints, epoxies—often cramming many different glass treatments into one project. Technical problems are no obstacle, neither impairing their vision nor bending their approach. Perhaps these are the people who are propelling American stained glass in a new direction.

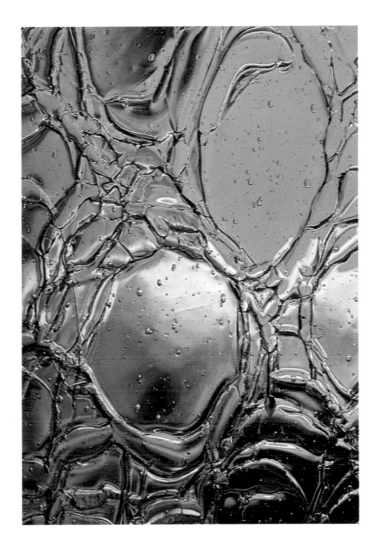

German-made crackle antique glass.

65

The Church of the Immaculate Conception in Everett,
Washington, houses these windows by Rambusch Studio.
The original design was abstract in form ; when the
congregation decided that it wanted something more
traditional, the artists painted these simple stylized
figures over the whole.

Temple Emanu-El, San Francisco. The honeycomb pattern of
the tracery acts as a support for this window, entitled
"Water." The artist, Mark Adams, ignored the tracery as a
design limitation and wove a tapestry of explosive color.
Shown above, a full view; on the facing page, a section.

St. Stephen's Lutheran Church, Granada Hills, California. This window by Roger Darricarrere was originally designed for the chapel at the New York World's Fair, 1964. When the fair ended, the congregation at St. Stephen's purchased the window and had it shipped to California and installed in their new sanctuary. Shown here, two sections ; on the facing page, a full view.

Above, a dalle glass window in the offices of Cornish & Carey, Palo Alto, California. Dalle is thick glass cut with a diamond saw and faceted with a carbon-tipped hammer. Many of the cuts in the above window are remarkable, in that it is difficult to cut an inside curve using the inflexible diamond saw. (Artist : Roger Darricarrere.)

Left, samples of dalle-de-verre *or dalle glass.*

*St. Michael's Church, San Francisco. The
color scheme of the dalle glass used here is
reminiscent of medieval glass windows.
(Artist : Gabriel Loire.)*

Temple De Hirsch, Seattle. A difficult structural framework for the glass artist : tracery which is not only geometric, but also closely-spaced. Here Darricarrere solved the problem by melding the design with the structure so that the grillwork disappears and the glass becomes an entire wall, almost of its own accord. Shown on this page, two details ; on the facing page, a full view.

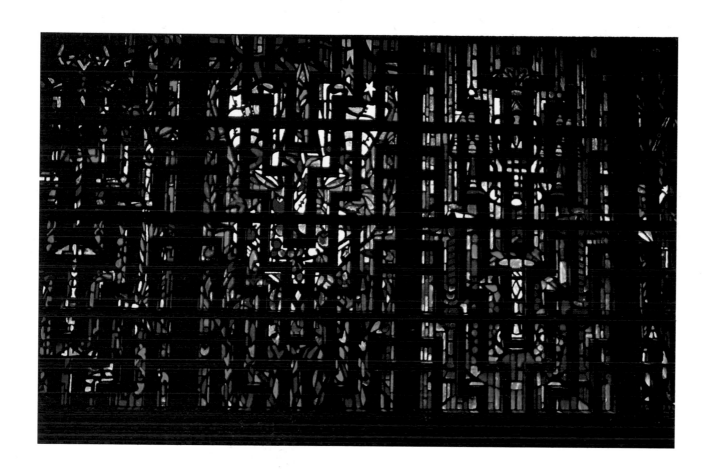

*Ezra Bessaroth Synagogue, Seattle, and
Warren State Hospital, Warren, Pennsylvania.
(Both windows and photos by Willet Studios.)*

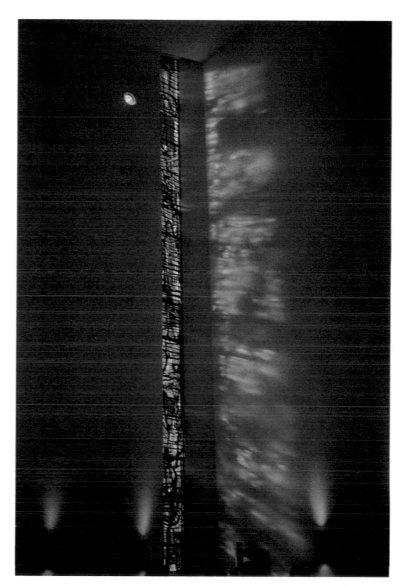

Above, Oak Hill Mausoleum, San Jose. The marble walls that flank this window reflect its colors. (Artists: the authors, with Brusey Studio.) On the right, St. Paul's Lutheran Church, Lititz, Pennsylvania. (Artists and photo: Willet Studios.)

On the left, the exterior of a concrete and dalle glass window. These are usually flat on both sides ; this one has an outside matrix built up in bas relief, following the contours of the window's design. (Bart Lytton collection.) Above, a dalle glass skylight in the Columbia Savings & Loan building, Los Angeles. (Both by Roger Darricarrere.)

The Museum of Science and Technology,
New York World's Fair, 1964. Above, an
exterior view ; to the right, a view from within.
To our knowledge this is the largest installation
of dalle glass in the world. (Artists and
photo : Willet Studios.)

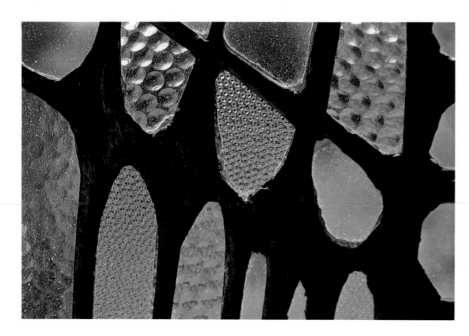

Mechanical glass, clear glass, and eye-glass lenses are combined here, using the copper-foil technique developed during the early twentieth century. Large gaps between the pieces are filled in with solder. (Artist: Joseph Veneski.)

Another Veneski window: mechanical glass and clear glass. At the artist's studio, Boulder Creek, California.

81

Detail of a window by Berkeley artist Peter Mollica, showing an interesting use of flashed opals, shower-door glass, and antique clear glass.

A design by Robert Sowers, hinting at the current German design trend. (Photo : Little Bobby Hanson.)

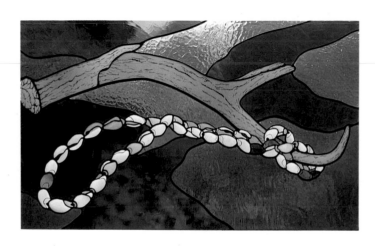

Leaded glass by Kathie Bunnell.

A window by Elizabeth Tallant.

84

A window by Elizabeth Tallant.

A section of a leaded-glass design, with a full view on the facing page. Artist Kathie Bunnell has achieved fine detail by the use of careful techniques.

*A single leaded window by Dan Fenton. Opposite : his
"Druid OakTree." (Both photos by the artist.)*

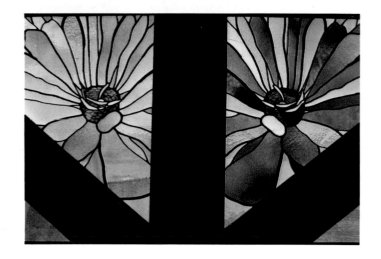

90

Above and on facing page : windows in a private residence in San Francisco. For the rose above, artist Quagliata used both acid etching and glass painting. A nice use of the variations of red.

Work in progress by Quagliata. The figure is done with silvered glass ; the surrounding glass is antique clear. In the detail above, the artist has used beeswax and tape to attach the work to a plate glass easel. In the photograph on the right, the panel is leaded but still incomplete.

92

In the sample above, glass paint was smoothed onto the surface of a red-orange glass, allowed to dry, and scratched away in a subtractive process. The piece was then fired to fuse glass and paint. (Artists : Finsterwald Studio.)

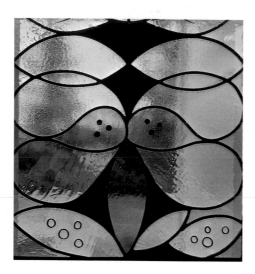

A private residence in Los Altos
Hills, California—leaded glass with
minimal use of glass paint. Above, a
detail; on the right, a full view.
(Artists: the authors, with Brusey
Studio.)

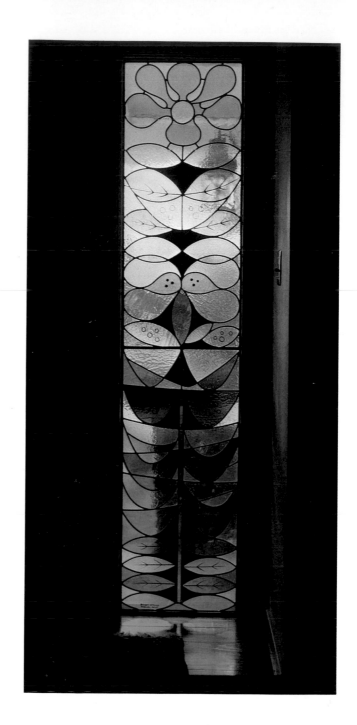

This panel by Seattle artist Bonnie Arnt combines photographic techniques with traditional leaded glass.

St. Louis Bertram Church, Oakland. To achieve this effect, artist Alberto Garcia Alvarez mounted unleaded glass on a glass easel and, using a long-handled brush, painted the glass spontaneously. The glass was then fired and leaded.

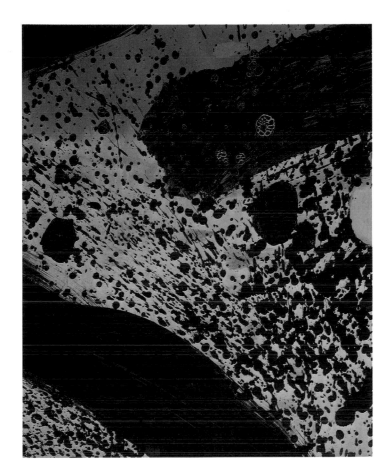

San Jose State University, San Jose—a chapel window done in laminated glass. Artist unknown.

St. Michael's Church, San Francisco.
A laminated glass skylight by
Robert Sowers.

99

Two examples of farbigem, a relatively new technique invented in Holland and further developed by Willet Studios. In farbigem, layers of glass are sandwiched together with resins. Above, Augustana Lutheran Church in Denver ; on the facing page, an in-studio farbigem ; both by Willet. (Photos by Willet.)

101

Left, and facing page, a window in a private residence in King City, California, done almost entirely in flashed whites, tinted whites, and opalescent whites, with colored antique glass along the bottom, and minimal glass paint (in the flower centers). The window is flanked with mirrors, giving the impression of endless corridors of stained glass. (Artists : the authors, with Brusey Studio.)

CONCLUSION

THE FINEST TRADITIONS of the stained glass craft are still very much alive, and the process involved remains basically unchanged. But the art as a whole has proved open to creative thought, and is beginning to gain status in its own right. The originality of the artists' efforts—their flexibility, their openness to changing concepts—suggests tremendous possibilities, for it is in this realm that the craft has not remained static. Stained glass artists can pursue their objectives with the expectancy of a deeper fulfillment than ever before, with greater assurance that their work will fascinate and encourage those who follow.

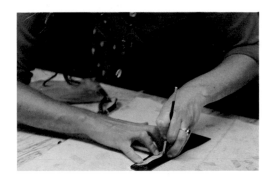

It is interesting that recognition of individual stained glass artists has always been practically nonexistent. During our travels, we have discovered hundreds of traditional and contemporary windows that were neither signed nor dated. We can only think that the labor of love and its resulting ethereal quality somehow transcend considerations of personal glory. Many of these dedicated artists work in relative obscurity, their efforts exhibited only in their architectural settings. Those who have become aware of stained glass are urged to seek out these works of art . . . to experience light and color as it travels through the eye and plunges deep into the mind, exploding in excitement.

PHOTOGRAPHER'S NOTE.   Any way you look at it, stained glass is strange stuff. It is a graphic art form executed in two dimensions, but it is viewed in three or even four. It has a contrast range from light to dark far broader than any other medium. And its colors can be incredibly saturated and full of sparkling texture. Those qualities must be carefully considered by both the designer and the appreciative viewer. To me, a photographer, it is a medium full of demanding photographic challenges.

When one medium confronts another, as photography does here with glass, allowances must be made. A photograph of a window can never reproduce the total effect of the living window itself. What the photographer can do, and should attempt, is to fuel your imagination; and perhaps, if a photograph is successful, you will see something which otherwise might have escaped you, even if you had been looking at the "real" window. In this book you see neither pure stained glass nor pure photography, but a sort of collaboration between the two. You see the way I saw these windows, and if you went to Chartres or Canterbury or the Baxters' house, you would see something different than I saw, perhaps very much different.

I use the still camera very much the way I use a motion picture camera: it moves in close for a detail, pulls back for a long shot, looks up at a steep angle. It is mobile, searching, inquisitive . . . because the process of studying anything visual is an active and individual process. It is my own sense of visual perversity that makes me point the camera at an odd angle to the surface of the glass, in order to include the sun in the shot, thus coaxing an aura or a sparkle from the window which the designer probably never considered, but which is there for your enjoyment if you'll make the effort to see it.

Three cameras were used to acquire the images: a Mamiya RB67, a Mamiya C330, and an old and trusty Nikon F. The Nikon is responsible for the bulk of the images, not for any special or technical reason, but because we know each other well after a lot of years and a lot of rolls of film.

I don't really consider myself a photographer; I am a filmmaker. In fact, this book is the direct result of the production of a film, "Stained Glass—Painting With Light," which I made several years ago. During the filming, Bob Hill remarked, "Hey, Hans, we ought to do a *book* about stained glass!" And so we did.

Paper for this book is Warren's Lustro Offset Enamel.

The typeface is Spectrum, set in Monotype by Mackenzie-Harris.

The book was printed by Carey Colorgraphic Corporation and bound by Roswell Bookbinding, both in Phoenix, Arizona.

Design: Frederick Mitchell and Judith Whipple with T. J. Parkes.